Danse Macabre

by

M. C. Rush

ISBN: 978-93-6354-568-7

First Edition: 2025
Rs. 200/-

Cyberwit.net
HIG 45 Kaushambi Kunj, Kalindipuram
Allahabad - 211011 (U.P.) India
http://www.cyberwit.net
Tel: +(91) 9415091004
E-mail: info@cyberwit.net

Printed at Repro India Limited.

Acknowledgments

I would like to thank the editors of the following journals and websites for first publishing some of the poems collected here.

Open Letters Monthly: "Enough"

Third Wednesday: "The Word 2"

These poems are for the ones who, finding them,
find they needed them.

Some, at least, of our loves commemorate
the sorrow not the joy of the world.
—William Bronk, "The Lack of Information"

Contents

Epic

I remember what we did for you and how appreciative you were
and how
our entanglement became a celebration around a final fire in which
burned
the broken bones of our enemies, our obstacles, our individual doubts,

and how we each contributed a flame to the fire, a spark to the light,
and a name to the roster of the champions of collaboration, of the
allied thieves
of victory, which we tasted and toasted together by the water
before parting,

before coming apart again into solitary heroes and villains and strangers
dispersing along expanding, diverging lines of newly-enriched lives,
each now lit,
each night, by an ember captured, carried away to linger for a while
or forever.

Anathematic

Do we need to know how we know what we need?

Or is it enough to want the sweet because it is sweet
without pretending it essential?

Needs that we don't desire are debilitating.
Desires that we don't need are distractions.

When specificity feels like understanding
we become beneficiaries of the hoax,

in the place where dreamers dream a similar dream,
connecting an outline of indications into an illustration.

The drunken donkeys of the day,
they bray, how uselessly they bray.

War born from lack of understanding
or bloody battles from too much.

Isn't what makes sense the sensible thing?

Propinquity

for our unique pattern
of errors chosen
from common option
praise isn't worth parsing
throw it into the fire
for a little extra heat
a little more light

too much light
too much darkness
and vision ceases
we are blind
algorithms of pain
looping, looping

hear the truth
in the echoes of falsity
intelligence and intent
energetic emissions of fitness
mortuary futility
myriad voices implying lying

the refracted rays of the sun
broadcasting alarm around
and through the cumulonimbus

Danse Macabre

The world may not be made of poetry
but consciousness is.

I sing the body eclectic
pretending a mind specific.

Arguing from and for our favorite constraints,
latent excellence.

Half the world wants it;
half the world wants to destroy it.

Even staying and sameness don't stay the same.
Hunger is the only ideology.

May you live in interesting times
without being interested in them.

If I were a dream,
whose dream would I be?

Androgenic

A supernumerary life lived
to set parameters,
establish preference,
compromised by habitual dreams of self,
discontent, the elixir, the poison,
buying ephemera,
burying essentials,
ostentatiously catbird
above the necessary intricacies.
Words seem into meaning
to punish pleasure with repetition.
Let me never be one of those
happiest without happiness,
saddest without sadness.

At Neap Tide

I am all the proof that everything can be nothing.
That the up close and impersonal.
The avoiding life at neap tide.

At times when I deny myself the power of denial
I will appreciate all that you have done as you
and in equal measure appreciate my undoing it.

As a poet, as a man, I can accept no constraint
upon my right to fall in love as often as necessary.
To harry myself into experience without metaphor.

Never trust anyone who doesn't love, or only loves.
There are somany things the words cando
and somany theycant.

And what would happen if I don't say enough
to see the truth?

How Many Ways

When life would bribe or threaten
me beyond endurance I would stand
on a smoking battlefield stacking corpses or
watch the dying dance through an earthquake
count a serial killer's trophies with him again
and again listen to the crash of cars sit
beside an empty polluted stream see all
the bodies sinking through the sea all
the fists and feet and weapons striking home
or try once more to smell the scentless camp gas.

How many ways can the world
say yes to no?

Cancer

Cancer cancers and,
cancering, cancels.
What can just enough
do with too much?
The taint defeats
inadequate constraints,
grows into go,
overflows into foe.
A question without answer,
asking, asking.
Cancers cancer to cancer,
to enhance the cancered
with error.
It's careless.

Sleep

The vista is obscured, so sleep.
The fog is on the ground, so sleep.
The sun goes up and down, so sleep.
The rain sings a sleeping song, so sleep.
The woes are circling round, so sleep.
The birds have flown away, so sleep.

The faces do not love, so sleep.
The voices are soft and far, so sleep.
The thoughts range farther still, so sleep.
The promises proved untrue, so sleep.
The memories don't pertain, so sleep.
The dreams are ever-sweet, so sleep.

You can't undo what has been done, so sleep.
You do not have to wake, so sleep.

Arbitrary

Take all your joys
and build a you.

All your sorrows,
another you.

Pit them against one another
for enough of eternity
that they fit again

or

every aspect of yourself
is dispersed like sand
in a storm.

Go

Go, get taken by every con,
fall for every trick.

Be fooled, foiled by everyone,
confused by everything.

Let all you have be stolen,
make every possible mistake.

Then, when you're done,
come back to me.

When all you had's gone,
come back to me.

If all that's left is pain…
I'm not waiting but I'm here.

Haunted

Ghosts haunt only bodies,
and only while they live.
Why murder your ghosts?
You are the haunted house
that children fear.
You are the haunted house
where things have happened.
You contain screams and moans,
which must be held somewhere
where they only occasionally get loose.

Without your ghosts
you become translucent
and hard to see.
The most important thing
is the gut-deep chill
as they enter you
to roam your halls
for your forever.

Following

When the sun came up I set out,
following a path that was called "the path."
The boss told me what I must do,
but it wasn't true
because I didn't do it.
The priestess told me a few things too
but I didn't listen to the priestess,
who was crazy, and wrong.
The machine asked me several questions,
but it was only humoring me
and I walked away from it.
It rained, then stopped.
I found food and drink.
I heard noises in the trees
but didn't investigate.
As the sun came down,
I returned again.
The machine asked me some questions,
but it didn't care about the answers
so I didn't answer.
The priestess cursed me
and said I was wicked,
but she was wrong.
The boss told me what I mustn't do,
but it isn't true
and I'll do it again
when the sun comes up.

A Crookneck Squash and a Honeybee

Spied on by bloody cherubs
we hang our laundry in the sun,
singing away the rain
that stained our neighbors' clothes
with the faraway joy and rightnow pain.

Love is undecorated; hate, ornate.
Beauty is not a proportion but a relation.

Chased by Cupid's scrimshawed fangs
we run from home and far away,
carrying a crookneck squash
and a honeybee.

Naked, naked, forced to flee
with a crookneck squash
and honeybee.

Translation from Anon

And they do things differently.
They don't think in riddles.
They don't speak in code.
They don't dream in poetry.
What doesn't eat them they eat.
What doesn't need them they need.
What doesn't want them—yes, they want it.
Not tutored in torture by authority.
Not dressed in duress.
They don't wait to die.
They don't rush to live.
They do things differently.
But still they do things.
That's the same.

Mostly

How simple life must have been
when there were only three or four paths.

Now there are millions, more, branching,
intersecting, deadending, looping, overlapping,
and we are more interested in the various maps
we make than in the actual routes we follow.

It's not what you have, it's what you want.
What you have to want.

How tedious life must have been
when there were only three or four narrow paths
and we walked them slowly, step by step,
until we fell.

What is done must.
What is doing mostly must.

Every Gift But

Give me every gift but finality
so I may continually add
to my collection of infinity.
Look at my collection! Use it, love it,
but remember that it's mine.
My world gets better (bigger?)
with everything you give me.
If I could give you anything
it would be the desire
to give me even more.

Progression

A poem is language.
Language is a pattern.
A pattern is a series of protocols.
A protocol is a series of procedures.
A procedure is a specified process.
A process is a series of choices.
A choice is the expression of purpose.
Purpose is the expression of preference.
Preference is based in precedence.
Precedence requires presence.
Presence is the result of power.
Power is produced from energy.
Energy is mainly position.
Position is perspective.
Perspective is prospect.
Prospect relies upon potential.
Potential is an expression of the possible.
The possible is a subset of language.
Language can express as a poem.

The Songs of the Tardigrade

Homo homini lupus est.

We will build new people
because none of us want to be
what we need from one another.
How many handshakes to mark the deal
that begins the end?

Pitting the profit motive against entropy,
what can life know of afterlife?
The universe only values life as an agent of change.
Erotic interrogations of quantum error engines.

Billions chanting low probability outcomes,
chanting the songs of the tardigrade,
chanting *stick your variable*
where your code don't compile.

The finite is always closer to zero than to infinity.

The Jester of Doomed Chances

How many times must I say
that Sisyphus and Narcissus are the same,
pushing the same reflection of the same face
up the same hill?

We approximate animal experience
(which is better than animals do for us).

Hitler is worse than Satan
(who has never done one thing on this earth)
but better than the aggregate darkness
of our apathy, our forgotten responsibility.

Authority must be opt-in.
Liberty must be opt-out.

And we dare congratulate ourselves
on resisting temptation into depravity?

The Austere Astute

surfeit of wit,
deficit of heart—
or the invert

the militant irritants of reverie,
the fecundity of perpetuity,
the most ambiguous atrocities

I need to see clearly
what we gain from simplicity
and what we gain from complexity

potency, poetry,
taking care not to veer into the merely earnest,
the bodyguards and blackguards of our least assessment

Diagnostic

Consciousness is, literally, a constantly-fading dream,
confronted with ghosts and other guests oblivious to the obvious.
It is hard to know and impossible to know for sure.
The last act of adolescence is the forfeiture of faith.

Is there anything harder to do well than live?
To demand equanimity is to expect a perfect execution.
There is no force in the universe strong enough,
savvy enough, to save us from ourselves.

The satisfaction of fall
stripped away by the coming of the cold.

Suizen

One. Another. A third.

Where nothing happens,
plenty happens.

Pulled from one end of myself to the other.

The river services the day.
The river services the second day.
The river services the third.

Infinity is infamous.

I shall bury my funeral
in my words.

A trace hints at a trail.

Nodes

All power, all presence
is based in ephemeral nodes.

Some mold the form of the world;
others prefer to incant content.

Euphemistic euphoria
complicit in complacency.

Most do their part
to impoverish a rich world.

All civilization is improvised
on the bones of those who could have mattered.

But drink of the hopeful waters
that underlie the rubble of ruins.

The world offers few butterflies
unencumbered by hungry caterpillars.

Emblems

For certain recursive iterations of self
rehearsing alternate histories,
alluvial illusions of continuity
confusing comprehensiveness for completion,
departure begins at arrival,
incarnation incanted into
the crass insistence on chance,
consequential commotions,
dispassionate dispossession,
and enigmatic emblems
of those who foul,
those who fail
to romance the lush,
banish the barren.

Are You Kidding Me?

All those killed in the camps
on the last day of the war?
Who crashed their car
before the divorce came through?
Who quit their jobs
eating retirement cake
or said their love
at the sides of graves?
Who breathed their last
in the waiting room?
Who followed the rules
and lost the game?
Who the hell's to blame?

New Stars

no outlaw
a quick enough draw
to best death
with his farmboy sickle

no horse or whore
loved enough
to ride
when the trail calls

no campfire
with enough sparks
to stir up
new stars

no frontier
wild enough
to de-face
the wanted posters

The Two

The man
who only needs what he wants
and the man
who only wants what he needs
meet
in the desert
under a disinterested moon:

Who needed it?
Who wanted it?
What will they say
to one another?

Which will sit beside the cholla
and sing
and which will lie down
and sleep?

Will the dream one dreams
outlive the song one sings?
What does the coyote think?

That The Mental Be Less Mortal

Theory has difficulty accounting for
what theorist isn't aware of.
Who or what qualifies as witness?
Probability only concerns itself with the possible.
Where is offsite experimentation being conducted
and who produces such malformula as
addition through subtraction, expansion
via contraction, focus from distraction?
Which palette, which spectrum, which
leparks and quartons, which clades?

What a distortion to call some stories
of some people the history of the world.
How much absolution there is,
or we see, in *change*.

Used To Be

Used to be
I would set my mind
to a thing
and do it.
But now I am
too small.
Now I set things
in my mind
and let them
grow.

Coral and Coal

How extreme should we be
in our position against extremists?
Can we demand the extradition of contrition?
When last we left our hero,
he…

Where you want to go
or believe you need to go
may lead you through
la Rue des Marionnettes Cassées
et Mannequins Brisées,

may lead you from
grotto to ghetto,
flags hung
like corpses
as warnings

(confusing composition with form
when form is composed of confusion,
these tedious cartoons
insisting to our faces
their precedence)

from the torturing tutors
of terror to those (us)
who want to *fight! fight! fight!*
but abhor war.
Or more war.

Bejeweled with coral and coal,
love begins some things,
will end everything,
in that moment
when security is breached.

Skeptical Spark

If time is granular
(if not truly annular),
and space is empty as far as it matters,
a vast void with a few lacy tatters
of mass, energy, and something unknown
whose unknowability we just can't condone
and so label "dark,"
as though we were the spark
bright enough to deduce
how it's all structured and what's coming loose
in a system ruled by entropy,
where dissolution is constant and yet things be,
then how can we possibly believe
that things are—only are—as we conceive?

The Inertia of Being

I know, by now, the kind of person I want to be,
and I see where I am and am not, a lot of where I will and will not,
and how thought needs shocks and surprises from the world,
from outside,
to elide its tendency to impart and repeat patterns of good enough,
rough templates for today, for we barely believe in today,
in the way we're confronted with challenge, with change,
that estranges our appreciation of our situation, and even less
in the mess of the mass of demands in the time to come,
some of which we can guess at but most of which we know
will show up unexpectedly to insist that we alter and adapt
to some crap that we hoped we'd miss or be better prepared,
and less scared, to rise above, or cope with, or endure,
and sure that as time passed and life went we'd at last
get past the inertia of being that keeps us from becoming ourselves.

I Believe

I expect that expectation will fail.
I want to want
that the work will work out,
but I fear that fear
and the needs of the needy
will pervert a perversion
of reward, rewarding
the desperate, whose desperation
drives them from the driven,
chases them from the chase,
leaving them to leave
the field to be fielded
by the losers and lost.
I believe that belief will fail.

Typical

Music for one, please.

Say typical.
Don't say normal.

Inhibiting habits
to hone the self.

The exacting transformations
required by continuity.

Not good enough for
but good enough.

Experience is never the same
as what's experienced.

Our cyclical apprehension
of our portion.

We fixate on aspect.

Past the Sale

How dumb was Zeus,
not to see Prometheus's long game?
You don't bring fire
without reason and caution
unless you intend destruction.
Call it power,
call it self-determination,
call it free will,
and turn it loose!

Stand back, here they come!

Voice & Chorus

A Voice: The difference between palace and prison
is power.

Chorus: Yer gonna die
gonna die
gonna die
o
yer gonna die
gonna die.

A Voice: The one who doesn't seek justice
can have no place in the society of people.

Chorus: Yer gonna die
gonna die
gonna die
o
yer gonna die
gonna die.

A Voice: The one who won't temper justice with mercy,
where appropriate, must also be cast out.

Chorus: Yer gonna die
gonna die
gonna die
o
yer gonna die
gonna die.

A Voice: We do what we're told,
what we tell ourselves.

Chorus: Yer gonna die
gonna die
gonna die
o
yer gonna die
gonna die.

If We Didn't Repeat

if we didn't repeat
if we didn't repeat
if we didn't repeat
we'd go too fast

if we didn't repeat
if we didn't repeat
if we didn't repeat
we'd go too far

if we didn't repeat
if we didn't repeat
if we didn't repeat
we might be something
but not what we are

[repeat]

Only When They Break

What makes the young unbearable
is the hope trapped in their earnest faces.
They aim for a world that never was,
will never be. You know
how they will punish themselves
for missing it. Only when they break
can we speak to them. Only
when they join us in the world-that-is
can we find them places in our grief
and show them small ways
of defending themselves against
the mad certainty of the young faces
about to pursue them, chasing them
toward the limits of tolerance.

Meaning

Meaning coagulates
in the wound of chaos,

in the dominant narrative
of child suicides,

the insistent assertions
of the assassinated,

the tyranny
of other nomenclatures,

of those content to not speak
of what doesn't insist,

in the efforts
of the executable world

to kill the immortal,
not the ephemeral.

The Missing Cheer

Loyalty is a strange concept.
Putting a commitment
above benefit.

Only the dead can afford
to be loyal,
for their interests
are greatly reduced.

Three cheers
("*Hear! Hear!*")
for the dead!

Host

More and more
I feel I'm a host
for words
that want to mingle and breed,
to engage and debate
with other words.

At first I thought
that wasn't much
of a life.
Now I think maybe it is.

This Thing

This thing or the other
that I feel
that they tell me
not to feel,
that they condemn me
for my unwillingness
or inability to stop
feeling, this thing
(or the other),
while not essential,
while less than optimal,
is still desirable,
still—I feel—defensible
while things aren't final.

It

It is alone in crowds and crowded in itself.
It seeks compatibility and confluence.
It avoids conflict and complaint.
It speaks enthusiastically in every language
    though it only understands or is intelligible in one.
It asks and asks of and asks for.
It tastes all the flavors
    and returns to those that arouse.
It walks in rain and through puddles.
It always and it sometimes and it never.
It does and it doesn't, can and cannot.
It starts and then finds it's done.
It remembers a bit, distorted, of what went before,
    and more that didn't.
It dreams that it dreams, even when awake.
It happens to be, and hopes to be happy.
It only knows now but lusts for forever.

Effect 2

When I am distracted and therefore mute,
the everything everywhere that doesn't know I exist
(if in fact I do exist) shivers
like the ghost of the future walked over the grave
injustice of its (all its) finitude.

When I am not saying what I have to say
(or can think to say), because I am distracted
or despondent or dependent (more dependent) upon hostile or
indifferent forces,
the atoms and their unknowable subcomponents stutter
and catch for the shortest instant of measurable time
with mechanical angst and automatic ennui
with no notion why their timeless cycles of call and response
have been interrupted (or indeed, most likely, usually, that they have).

My silence goes unheard but is not without effect.

No One

when
when no one
when no one is left
when no one is left who understands
when no one is left who understands your code
shares your mode
remembers your road
when no one is left who knew you when
no one is left who knew
no one is left
no one
then
alone
begin
again

The First Morning

On the first morning
after my last day,
let the sun shine
and the rain fall
and the wind blow.

Let the clouds drift
and the cats nap
and the dogs play.

Let the trees stand
and the bees hum and
the birds dart with delight and purpose,

though I have no more purpose
and the birds and bees and trees
and wind and rain and cats and dogs
have already forgotten me
and the sun never knew me.

O, beautiful morning!

The New Year Ends A Year Of Sorrow

—after Cold Mountain

the new year ends a year of sorrow
the new year begins a year of joy
joy is sorrow discovered
sorrow joy become familiar

knowing there are no endings without beginnings
we believe there must be endings for there to be beginnings
as though all-that-is didn't laugh at our limits
everything is the same and then it isn't

laugh at your limits
weep at your lack of time to overcome them

Jou-yen

Without memory, no identity.
Without identity, no memory.

From all that we have
we select what we want.

Calculating
(and then contemplating)

the implications
of occasion.

All who see me,
tell me one true thing.

Retrieve me
from this cloud of lies.

The illusion of plenty doesn't feed the hungry.
The illusion of scarcity doesn't fool the savvy.

I Do

What is
doesn't require
me to acknowledge it

but I do.

What was
doesn't require
me to remember it

but I do.

What will be
doesn't require
me

but I do.

What I Had

I want what I had
for what I have is less,
though more than it will be.
Living, we learn to relish
a shrinking self, and to love
what left over what's left
as we reduce.

Not better and better
forever, and cursed
with remembering
what we were before.

Merrily, Merrily

Life starts out
vivid and unexpected as dream,
but we demand it relent, compel it
to capitulate, to hide its strangeness
from us,
to seem
sensible, straightforward, and true—
only seem, for all the while
it continues, behind the scenes we choose to view,
as unknowable in content and style
as the logic we lie about.

Who Can Rest

Who can rest
when there are palaces to raze,
gardens to uproot,
orchards to cut down,
libraries to burn?
When there are yet treasures to loot,
herds to slaughter,
crops to destroy?
When there are heirs to kill
and maidens to violate
and sages to banish?
Who can hold,
who can quit,
when there are still
promises to break
and lies to tell
and beautiful things
crying to be undone?

The Fruit

the fruit
of the tree
of the knowledge
of good and evil
tasted bitter
tasted bad—
that was the lesson
that the knowledge
that other fruit was better
and that forevermore
we'd privilege preference
cater to desire

That Thing There

That's beautiful,
that thing that you have,
that thing that you hold
there in your hand.
What will you do with it,
and where can I get one?
(I won't ask for that one.)
My hand has grabbed, gripped,
held so many things but still
feels so empty.

How—I don't understand—
have you managed to hold beauty?
Where are you taking it, and would it
frighten you if I followed you?

All The Things 2

Of all the things I could have done, this?
Of all the things I wanted to get, that?
The embassies of embarrassment
keep sending tall gentlemen in dark ties
and efficient women with reasonable demands,
but I've left standing orders to turn them
away. Their diplomatic immunity
doesn't entitle them to a seat at the table
when negotiations begin over
assigning responsibility
for all the things.

Life's Catalog

Life's catalog is so rich,
its delivery charges so steep.

Ignorance dares more than courage.
Enthusiasm for the unnecessary.

Things happen for a reason.
And the reason is that things happen.

Better a dozen sharp sorrows
than one that settles and strangles.

If nothing interfered with us,
what would we be?

Is our everything nothing
against the nothing we know of everything?

Should we ever master partial,
shall we get a peek at whole?

The Hero's Journey

Say no, but never say never.
Doubt even doubt.
Celebrate even cursory infatuation.
Evade sumptuary restrictions
on cognitive relations.
Recognize those who like epiphany
and those who like anecdote.
Nothing is
divisible by hero.
We must reject must.
Possibility may be moral;
certainty never can.
They promised us a reckoning
but all we get is an ending.

Incompatible 2

Are we the pattern
or the organizing principle?

There is very little to essence.
Most everything is decoration.

The world fits into me
better than I fit into the world.

Sensation is a limitation
that may guide us to infinity.

Suffering is the weapon
we use against oblivion.

The instant you believe,
you're deceived.

Identity is incompatible
with freedom.

Enough

There's enough of the world
to last my whole life,

not enough of my life
for the whole world.

But that's not the point.

I am here and I am there
but truly I am here-and-there.

(What, man?
We all contain waltitudes.)

Not of course but oh wow.

What dies is the illusion of continuity,
appetite is eternal enough.

The world doesn't need everyone
to win.

Is and Does

I'll make a story of all the first times
and a poem of all the last times
and put them in a book and call it *My Book*,
though it's not my book, not a chapter,
not a word, it's plagiarized from everyone else
plot, setting, and theme, and who would write this,
who would write this,
when any word could mean anything,
and does,
and anyone could be anyone,
and is?

Will I?

I can still do it.
I just have to go slower,
be a little more careful.
No, I have to go faster,
be less cautious!
No longer time for that.
No longer time for this.
I don't know if I can do it,
if I could ever have done it.
I am my time, and I am
deflating like a balloon.
And soon, soon…
I will be less able,
I will be less. I am less.
I will be even less.
What, then, will I do?
What do I do now?
What am I doing?
Why have I done it?
Why haven't I done it?
Can I still do it?
Do I still care
enough? Does anyone?
Is it worth it?
Is there time? Will I?

Up To A Point

Can there be a soul without a self?
Or is it preposterous?

I am the kind of question,
he said, that can't be improved

by an answer.
But don't let that stop you.

Always ask.
Always answer.

To think is a useful trick.
Up to a point.

This is the sound
of one man napping.

It's hard to deal with people
only intermittently intentional.

Nothing But

I'm a'tell you what, Brother Money,
sweating and swatting, I'm a'chastize
the sun for coming up wrong,
beauty
polluted,

and I'm a'pray,
cuz curses, too, are prayers.
What's the matter?
The matter is what matters.

We grow nothing but impatient.
We make nothing but trouble.
We build nothing but ruin.

Ah, Brother Money, the enormity of the world
in the mind of a child.

Memories of Memories

Life is no reward
and death no punishment.

You can't make me care.
You can't make me stop caring.

We love what is a little strange.
What is a little strange is a little familiar.

Love is exclusive.
I mean, love is exclusion.

Alone, not with memories
but with memories of memories.

For every inaction there must be
an equal and opposite inaction.

Life is no punishment
and death no reward.

A Record

A hole, a tear, a crack, a dent,
a cut, a gash, a break—some other wound—
an injury is there forever,
though it may heal or seem to heal.
It's wholeness, perfection, the undamaged
that is rash, that strains credulity and patience,
that seeks to persuade us, to deceive us,
that we are other than we are:
a record of change and harm,
imposition and recovery. Renewal.
We feel each hurt, and suffer it,
often unconscious of its lasting effect:
at times we only come together
after we've been wrecked.

The Path Ahead of Me

The path ahead of me is beaten down,
the weeds and grasses trampled,
the creeks and pools mostly dried up or drunk,
and the air lightly-scented with smoke and soot.
I follow where before me went
countless raccoons, elephants,
otters, tigers, nymphs, poets,
and soft-pawed cats.
The sun sets or rises,
the moon waxes or wanes,
the tide ebbs or flows
as I walk and sometimes run
ahead behind the others
to see if I can ever catch them.

The Old Church

I visited a shiny pew
to listen to the fading echoes.
I examined the empty altar
and imagined all the sacrificial crumbs of yesteryear.
I walked through the shady cemetery
and marveled at how so many
had wasted their lives.
If only they had put their faith in libraries.
If only they had read instead of prayed.
If only they had dreamed bigger
than their father.

The light streaming through the stained glass—
what an effect!

The light through the leaves dappling the stream, too.

Destiny 2

This is what we wished for
when we were eukaryotes,
when we were fish.
Each time we dream
we dream bigger.
With each bigger dream
we get bigger.
Now we imagine
we imagine everything,
and imagine becoming everything.
We swim like sperm
to become.
Destiny is where you arrive,
not where you intended to go.

Akimbo

I see the corpses beckon
though they just lie akimbo,
a symbol of a summoning
of the quick to dust.

The chamber of ten thousand skulls
requires the manufacture and application
of twenty thousand eyes.

Your signal calls me to you,
even your warning signals.
What is it that makes me approach
coherence where I'd ignore or avoid noise?

There are two kinds of equality:
where everyone matters
and where no one does.

Everything is conspiring
to make you notice,
to make you care
that everything is conspiring.

One Bird

Choose one bird
of all the birds
that ever were.
Are you sure?
That bird?

Pick one star
of all the stars that are.
Or no longer are.

A blade of grass, a tree, a leaf.
A cloud, a drop of rain, a grain of sand.

How minuscule
your favorite molecule.
How absurd.

One bird.

The Amnesiac

Don't look back,
as though temptation were all
that remains behind.
But everything—*everything*—is there!
More than mere resource,
what's over our shoulder *is* us:
citation of memories
of past action. If we don't reverse
focus from time to time we are blind
not only to the histories
that made us and the forces
that drive, guide us,
but to the untended consequences
that stalk the amnesiac.

La Belle Mort

Only for people
are dead things beautiful.
We, who struggle so
with an ugly world,
want to be beautiful when dead.
Beginnings come
to tire us with their endlessness,
with the sameness of their
naive repetitions, and so
we turn our attention, our allegiance,
to endings, and to ending.
What dies, what up and leaves,
and leaves the living to suffer
our cares, first startles, then numbs.

Locus

The universe is grand,
but we love best what's at hand.

We love
what we see
even when we know
how much it keeps
us from seeing,
from knowing.

We love our focus,
fastened in our locus.

The Truth 3

There is truth.
There is the telling of truth.
Which is bigger?
Which is better?
Is bigger better?
Is better bigger?
I am a lie
who loves the truth
and the telling.
And I'm telling you,
that's the truth.

Working As Intended

The flaws, the fails;
the excess, the waste;
the effort and indolence;
the errors and reluctance;
the average, the aggregate,
and the deviation;
the doubt, the assurances,
the delusions;
the false starts, the premature ends,
hope, fear, need;
instinct, habit, drive, urge,
the ceaseless hunger, the chances to feed.
A billion billion nodes
interacting in a trillion modes.

Rorschach & Escher

I begin to suspect
that we have attributed
too much to too many.

Forgive it. Forgive each.
But in forgiving each
must one forgive all?

I pity (and fear) those
who hear *change* and think *death*.
But rather than admire mere achievement
I would set tasks to who set tasks to Hercules.

Our brief acquaintance
with everything
provokes much commentary
but little understanding.

Under Pressure

I have to start a lot.
I have to finish everything.
Because the end is coming
and may arrive at any time.
The end, which will make irrelevant
what I started and what I finished.
The less time left,
the more I must do,
the less I can delay, deny.
Squeeze a tube from one end,
more pressure builds at the other.
Give everything very little time, very
little attention, and the world shatters,
nothing matters.

The Coyote's Howl

Thoughts are not rational but symbiotic.
Certainty is riddled with ambiguity,
reason, another dream
of the mythologies of self,
the fantasies of unity, of identity,
everything a sign of every other thing,
symbols infinitely networked in interdependence.

Devoted to a map
of all the accidents of the moment,
nigh-infinite hypotheticals
directed and constrained
with if-then provisions,
memory as subset of personal history,
you may end up in poor company or alone.

Between the cliche of the coyote's
howl and the coyote's howl: a place
(or at least a space)
we can visit but never colonize.
What if our sense
that the emptiness shouldn't have us
is baseless?

How much allowance should be made
for what we are
that we shouldn't be?
Attraction. Aversion.
Transition.
Echoes lack intent, and so lack intent to mock,
and yet, feeling mocked, we are mocked.

Hummingbird.

Occlusion

Support love or support knowledge;
the one occludes the other.

We cherish the particular
accidents we encounter.

We can attribute anything to anyone,
make villains of heroes and martyrs of monsters.

Too often I condemn what you do
to justify what I do (including the condemnation).

We must find those
whose words seem plausible.

Meet weakness with dismay,
greet power with disdain.

It is true and it is not true.
That's the best that I can do.

What To Do 2

Some things are preferable to others
in certain contexts
based on certain criteria.

Some criteria are preferable to others
in certain contexts
based on certain preferences.

And there's the problem of what to do
with all of the data
that comes after the decision.

What we want is to be frozen in an eternal
state of readiness, with all choices apparent
yet unchosen.

Need is earth; desire, fire;
life is air and death is water.

The Magnificent Obsessions

The imposition
of coherence,

the antimentalist's
defensive inattention,

the autotelic wordplay of
perceptual emotion machines,

those who shout *Dire!*
in a crowded theater,

symbiotic symbols
for regressive barbaradigms,

the trash you place upon your altars,
the solipsistic murder urge.

We will invent gods, but first
we will invent ghosts.

Frozen

A princess, he said. A penguin.
He stopped. One eye pleaded
for understanding. The other hid.
It rained, he said.
Sky gray, he said.
The streets drained the city
and the soil drained the valley.
Then everything slowed.
The water slowed so
it froze.
So it goes, I said,
glancing at the sky.
But why, he said.
Why he said a penguin
when he surely meant a princess
I don't know.
He was old.

Tribunal

The ancients did some things
well which matter not at all
or to us. And slowly we came
to the things we do, and one is to
neglect and then abandon one
for another that seems to better suit
or fit what we decide are our requirements
or what we see we need we didn't see
before. We do some things well
which few or none have done as well
before or will again, it's certain, and others
so poorly as to appall tribunals toward eternity,
who, doing some things well, will elevate
condemnation of some things we've done.

Others 2

Others are not far from us
but too far.
We look upon them
looking and weeping
and weep.

We reach for them—
their hands are definitely
waving or reaching—
it's no good. It's bad.

We love ourselves
to show them how
we would love them
if we could have them,
if they were close enough.

And How Does the State of the Economy Relate to the Well-Being of the Individual?

Rather than these efficient mobs
that enter, dismantle our lives, and depart,
let us pretend that we are undone
by remote ideas hinted at half in jest,
by scales which diminish us to insignificance,
by general truths which accrete to quiet
our specific idiosyncrasies.

Concealed here, there in voided landscape,
that which appeases our outrage
at being used so,
at being so used.

Myths, too, seek the flame.
The only thing we have is experience,
and we don't get to keep it.

An attempt to respond to my age

the simple beauty of the simple
the complex beauty of the complex
we nest adjacent to identity
more hole than whole
you're soaking in it
the already-assimilated
the almost-all-simulated
schismatic schematics
teaching us to adore the ambiguous face
to embrace generic beauty
our math fails to show
how all change is unchanging
if I hadn't known better
I'd have known better

to laugh without mirth
to weep without sorrow
without basis for bias
it's where you put the stress
what isn't there
shapes our appreciation of what is
as aspiration feeds accomplishment
as thwarted intent
what we can't heal
what we can't heat
put us where all is wrong
and we'll struggle to belong
the simple truth of the simple
the complex truth of the complex

Assertion 3

Blinded by vivid imagery
to how much is essential but not important
we insist on experience.

The prior thing strove for next,
the next thing longs for prior.

There are always more to liberate,
there is always more to be liberated *from*.

We'll destroy the world
to chastise ourselves.

We tell stories to try to see
a world made of something
other than story.

Assertion
can be beautiful.

Ahead

I awake
a head
and roll
away
singing
and tasting
the ground.

At last
I pass
someone
listening.

All Dancing

to begin to dance, to dance on,
knowing the dance must end

knowing all dancing will end

to let the music arise through the flesh
to let the flesh move to the music

knowing all dancing will end

to look a partner in the eye
to try to find a spontaneous smile

knowing all dancing will end

to dance with a mirror
to dance with a shadow

knowing all dancing will end

to spin and to shake
to strut and to shimmy

knowing all dancing will end

to dance and to dance and
to dance and to dance

knowing all dancing will end

Bumfighting in the Graveyard

Bumfighting in the graveyard
with the freshest corpses—
fresh enough to remember anger,
to feign injury,
to mimic pain,
betting on winners
among these losers
who lumber and lurch
in their soil-stained finest
and throw a sort-of punch,
aim an almost-kick, at anything,
at any body, that stumbles into them,
silently striking out
at the world they left behind.

Reverse Apotheosis

Look, the word word is a useless word.

I imagine names for you that are not words,
then must settle for writing of you with words that are not names.

How much cold
to contain the heat
of a trillion stars?

Denounce your words carefully.

I still believe (ha!) there is a responsibility to blaspheme
against the most precious lies, the most cherished dream.

There are times when I simply cannot pronounce others' words
or parse their grammars. Perhaps I try too hard,
for it is not too difficult, usually, to intuit their meaning
if one ignores their own heart-dealt interpretations
and remembers the nature of human nomenclature.

Your wordless sounds
now your wordless silence
giving rhetorical answers.

We love nonsense
stated with certainty.

At least
at last
kiss.

Eyelids rubbed gray
with the ash of burned love letters.

Oh look, the lacuna between the first WORD
andthefirstsentence.

The first thought
when you get what you wanted
is *Should I have wanted more?*

The Desperate Inessentials

All the things
slipping through the human world
human-created, human-valued, human-preserved,

household gods shattered on sturdy
almost-level hearths by heathens
and the hopelessly devout.

What seems to matter
isn't always what matters.

Contemplate the space,
itinerant thinker:

What once was is,
yet benefits not from being

or

where one was,
none is.

Nothing matters.
Everything matters.
Scale is all.

Other interpretations are possible.

Expiating Wins

"Superlatives have lost most of their charm."
—Samuel Beckett, from "Texts for Nothing"

creak followed by crack,
derogatory derivatives
of governing oratory

synaptic fornication
appropriately propitious
mixolydian
artisanal paleographics

culture is indefensible,
what others deem
worth museuming,
the next god to go down

better idle than idiot
estranged from the strange,
the eventually evident

we piss on what thirsts,
shit on what hungers,
and take credit for every iota of growth

everyone stitched to a shadow
shroud and told to go
their own way and be
a little merry

to deny even
the certainty
of the cemetery

well, why not?

Call

Call me
not with my name,
for what is my name,
but with the name I was meant to have,
the name of what I was meant to be,
of something I could have been
other than what I am,
or the name of what I thought I was,
thought I was becoming,
thought I would at some point turn into
but haven't.

Call in a way that I can hear and respond to
without having to justify who I am
or who I am not. But call.

Forward March

I too have built, am building,
terra cotta soldiers to carry my past
and accompany me through life
and into death. But I know they will all,
every hundred thousand, every million,
stop at the cliff while I continue over,
stop and stand, sightlessly, silent,
without movement, until the inevitable
becomes acceptable, until the bottomless
canyon begins to echo unfathomable songs,
until what is forgotten is remembered again,
remembered so well and with such love
that everything is as it was
and does as it did. Until then.

Admit Impediment

If we are not to wed
then let our dream of perfect bliss lie dead.
Let us move from joy to joy,
passing quickly through the voids,
enjoining sense and thought
to gather what can be from what is not;
and let the lie that others chase,
of permanence and grace,
their fantasy and guiding fiction,
no longer define our addiction
to one another
and to the two of us together.
I won't seek heaven in you, you won't find it in me.
Going forward, for our happiness, we'll just let all things be.

Palimpsest

Every prince should leave his palace.
Seek the desert within the desert,
the oasis within the oasis.
Magician, alchemist, sage, holy fool,
philosopher, scientist, child, idler, dabbler.
Our destiny is to be greater than our destiny.
How intolerable thistles without a bloom!
The anxiety of childhood is what is not known.
The terror of adulthood is what is.
Life is what we do while we await execution.
We overwrite what is there
when we care or don't care.
Leave his palace for others.
Freedom enslaves us to opportunity.

What I Found

What I found
wasn't what I expected,
wanted.

Well,
hell.

Now what
do I do with it?
Shit.

Really,
this is unsatisfactory.

I think
I'd like
another look.

To search this mess
for something else.

Look 3

So much effort
to get us to look
here and *here*.
Don't.
Look where it seems
there is nothing to look at.
Where nothing is happening.
Look away from
the bright light,
the loud noise.
Look where you'd never
think to look,
where no one is looking.
And keep looking.

An Economy

Was and was and was is am.
Will be is a dream. I will wear
no insignia if I have to go bare.

Nor fetishize my infirmities.
Some concessions, yes,
but no. Not those.

When patterns fail,
we abandon patterns
and, ultimately, pattern.

Marrying the arbitrary,
we are almost immediately
shaken by our incompatibility.

Our ambitions, our drive,
may require an economy
that pays for what we don't do.

And When They're Gone

When they're here
they're mostly going.
Eyes on
the horizon.
Listening to the wind.
They know what's coming,
more or less.
They smile. They try.
They mean well.
But you can tell.
They know
it's time, or almost time,
to go.
And so.

The Word 2

In the beginning was the cry,
the laugh and the cry, the gasp,
the sigh, the sniff, the snort,
the inhalation of revelation
and the exhalation of disappointment.
The word came much later. The thing,
the sensation, the provocation, the reaction,
even the *thought* came before the word—
a sort of thought, unexpressed, built
of twitch, affinity and association,
of recognition and comparison,
a representation of perception.
The word came later, to create
and then endlessly rework history.

To The Weary

I, too, tire, am tired, of this world.
And I do not say that grief is brief or life is but a dream.
But, unlike so many who also sleep each night,
I haven't forgotten the purpose, the promise, of rest.
Tomorrow, whatever it may be, will not be today.
You will find yourself elsewhere, among others,
and changed. There will be opportunities
for new sorrows, new regrets, which may be lighter,
more easily carried, than these. Something you have
never seen or even imagined may save your life.
Your body, without prompting, may suddenly surge
with the enthusiasm of youth, restored, renewed,
and it may be that, after rest, you may remember
why it used to seem worthwhile to try.

Leave It

If you can't take it with you,
then leave it all behind, everything
you make, everything you find.
If you can't keep it with you,
then toss it all away, everything
you love, if you can't make it stay.
Tear it off and cut it loose
until there's little left—you must
even release the itch to feel bereft.
We try to carry so much more
than our strength permits.
Now it's time to say, enough,
just this, this is it.

Not Yet

I will break.
I will be ruined.
I will die.
But not yet,
oh, not yet!
I will stop.
Be destroyed.
And I'll die.
But not yet!
I'll no longer be I,
no longer be me,
I'll no more be.
But not yet!

Dolorem Ipsum

I would like to know an untroubled soul.
I would like to meet a sweet visage.
To find someone living a contented life.
To see someone at peace without being oblivious.
Untouched by disappointment and resentment.
Unbroken by expectation and injustice.
For whom kindness is still the first impulse.
To whom pain hasn't become chronic.
Who still delights in all things.
Who hasn't retreated into panic, suspicion, or delusion.
Who doesn't burn with regret for what they've done and didn't do.
Who wakes eagerly and goes to sleep easily.
Who yet looks, listens, thinks, and tries.
Still in love with the whole damned thing.

Of the Telling of Tales

If the sun is the god and the moon is the ghost
and we have abandoned our quest for the campfire
and for the telling of tales of our quest around the campfire
(and then the telling of tales of the telling of tales)
and the poking of coals with a great green stick
to provoke galaxies of sparks which can't compete
with the god or with the ghost but vastly outnumber them,
(which is a different kind of superiority,
one we carry in our history and in our loins),
and if doing is a kind of showing
and showing a kind of telling,
and so everything we are capable of,
lurking, looking,
collapses into a hot toxic breath
expelled into the air of the god
and the air of the ghost
as an enumeration of our multiplicity,
as a naming of our specificity,
then that which darkness brightens
and bright darkens unwittingly or unwillingly
demonstrates a bias toward the obvious:
that what is erased is order, what is removed is structure,
drained by the imperceptible perplexities to a cryptic resistance;
that while the frenetic sparks and the fanatic makers of sparks,
ambiguously ceremonial, celebratory, are dazzled
by phenomena then distracted by interpretation,
the light need not defeat the darkness,
only discover a space within it to illuminate.

The Knob of the Door of the Never-Could-Be

I admire the view of things as they are,
the truculent, desperate, determined, so vast.
I watch each one as it rushes past.

I politely acknowledge things as they might be,
nod to the wild and swollen, the fevered and bettered, the fallen.

But my hand's on the knob of the door
of the never-could-be, and when next I've an instant
I'll turn it and enter and shut it behind me.

I'll shut it behind and be seen no more.
I'll open, and enter, and then close that door.

If I Had Never

If I had never drawn a breath
If I had never seen the light
If I had never tasted anything
If I had never held a hand
If I had never slept and woken
If I had never tried
If I had never failed
If I had never resisted
If I had never consented
If I had never changed
If I had never remained the same
If I had never written a poem

Easily

We die so easily,
are so easily killed.
Like the sun comes up every morning,
as easily as that.
Like the rain gathers and falls,
as easily as that.
Like a rock sits and waits,
as easily as that.
We are so easily killed
and kill so easily,
like the wind moves,
like the wind stops moving.
As easily as that.

I Remember 2

I remember things from long ago
and I remember recent things
and I remember them the same,
but only certain long ago things,
most I have forgotten,
and not recently, I mean,
I didn't remember them
and so I don't.

But I do remember things,
of course I do, and all the same,
and while storage and retrieval
and rehearsal take time,
the memories I've taken out
of time, and they all happen together
now, to the extent that they happen now,
and not in time but stripped of time,
and I don't remember the process
of converting things to memories of things,
and I'm a thing, a thing that remembers
things, and when I can no longer remember
a thing my memory of the thing
will not revert to the thing,
and when I can no longer remember,
I will not revert to anything
but will be taken out of time
and recent and long ago
will not happen together

and (some) things will reemerge
as memories of things fade.

I won't be one of those things.

Hearing Voices

The voice of silence and the voice of noise,
the voice of assertion and the voice of dissent,
the voices of others and the voices of self,
the voice of doubt and the voice of conformity,
the familiar voices and the voices strangely whispering,
the strong voice and the tentative,
the voice of reason and the voice of madness,
the welcoming voice, the rejecting,
the loving voice, the raging,
the beloved voice, the grating,
the idle voice, the voice of industry,
the reassuring voice, the questioning,
all speaking, speaking.
Or not speaking.

After The Humans Did What They Did

The birds flew away.
One by one, in pairs,
flock after flock they flew off.
Took stock and said *Enough*,
and left.

The sky cried
at their departure,
but the sky always cries.

The worms rose to the surface
and prepared to feast.
Birds said no
and worms said yes.

And you can bet those birds left
no forwarding address.

What I Want When It Happens

When the wind wakes,
I want to run. To run away.

When the sun hides,
I want to walk along a broken road.

When the rain burns,
I want to listen without understanding, then sleep.

When the people fight,
I want to move into the trunk of a tree.

When the old die,
I want to stack a stone on anther stone.

When the ice melts,
I want to wash my hands and eat.

When the creek dries,
I want to play charades with the last fish.

A Page

Let us play with words until they become
so serious we can't stand it and then
let us erase them, some of them, a few
of them, and then let us play with the words
that are left, say the words that are left,
and when they mean nothing to us,
when they barely connect to us,
let us write them, let us right them,
let us make something of ourselves
making something of them, and let us
take what we make and raise it,
praise it for being unserious, for saying
what can be said rather than what needs to
be said, and each carry a page into the storm.

Too Late

Already it is too late to see the world.
Everywhere is man man man.
Dig a pit in the ground, higher than your head,
and stand in it during a thunderstorm.
That's as close as you'll get.
People have beautiful ideas,
but they are incompatible with the world.
The skin of your body will be chilled
by the cold water.
It's too late, too late,
and here you are.

A Little Something

Leave a little something on my stone,
something precious but not dear.
Take in exchange the promise
of a blessing I can't deliver
but which you deserve.
I've given all I had to give.
Now I'm alone.
So thanks for reading this,
though I'm not here.
Now think! Feel! Live! Be!
Before you too are done like me.

These Days

Lengthen each of my days
until they become tedious and slow,
until they snail forward and barely move at all.
Let each day last a month.
No matter how rested I wake,
let me collapse finally into bed exhausted.
Let each day last a year.
Let each day be an expedition
to capture the horizon.
Let me make of each day an entire memoir.
Let each day last an era.
Because these little days that I'm left with
now have barely a minute in them,
yet still they count against me.

A Poem

I'd like to write a poem on every continent,
in every country, in every city, every town.
Along every street, in every alley, standing,
sitting, lying down on every corner, every
intersection. In the arms of every woman.
At the side of every man. And on the moon.
Under every tree of every forest, with my feet
dangled in every river and stream, my head
bobbing on every sea, swimming and sinking.
At every hour of day and night, at every position
of the sun in the sky, and one for every cloud,
for every thought I have, every dream, and
for every cell struggling in my body, in every body.
Robust with health, and suffering every illness.
I'd like to write a poem for every poem I write.
But maybe one would be enough.

The Theory

The theory is we've become more conscious,
but what if we've become less?
As copies of copies of copies,
how sure are we of our fidelity?
We look forward now and imagine
making AI indistinguishable from us
in every measurable way and yet lacking.
What if we also lack something
we can't ourselves detect without an original,
or a baseline, a standard, to match? What if
thousands of years of almost good enough
wasn't good enough? What if
our sense that something is missing
means something is missing?

And Then

And so I end this poem.
But then something I forgot to say.
And then a better way to say something I said.
And then something I didn't know then.
And then a clearer illustration of a point.
And then a stronger illumination of a theme.
And then a great new word.
And then an essential line.
And then something that seems to fit.
And then something strange I really like.
And then something that adds a whole new dimension.
And then something that confuses the issue.
And then the removal of everything I can live without.
And then the putting back of everything I love.

The Forgotten Idol

The idol, buried in a hundred years of wind-litter
(or more!), was carved blind and never saw a thing.
Never felt pity or mercy, though it may have dimly detected
lichens perching on its skin. Sheltered from the sun
as first the shrubs and then the trees grew back,
sinking slowly into ground softened by a century of rain
(or more!), the stone that never knew it was other than a stone
(not even that, only stone) was visited by insects, snakes,
the occasional venerating bird, but lay unseen by those
closest to him who made it, who put his skill in the service
of faith or fear, or otherwise schemed to profit
from shaping shapelessness into hope, to stand or sit upon
the ground a hundred years (or more!) beyond the day he fell.

An idea turned to stone confounds the living brain,
for which any pretense at permanence will always seem bitter.

www.ingramcontent.com/pod-product-compliance
Lightning Source LLC
LaVergne TN
LVHW091059150826
845673LV00002B/646

* 9 7 8 9 3 6 3 5 4 5 6 8 7 *